Little Healers® Guided Meditation

Written by Becky Payne

Illustrated by Moran Reudor

For my son, Levi,
you are my warrior.
You've got the sweetest parts of my soul.
I hope you always embrace both aspects of yourself and
teach others to do the same. I love you with all of my heart.

In this guided meditation book, you will find simple meditations that are ten minutes or less to share with your whole family. This book is for parents or caregivers to read to their children; perhaps someday, their children can read it back to them.
You could also use this in a classroom setting!

When mindfulness is taught from birth, it becomes part of how your child lives their life, not something they have to do every day; it is just part of the day.

Teaching babies and children this vital coping skill is one of the greatest gifts you can give them. By teaching them meditation, you show them how to heal themselves and care for themselves. You are laying a foundation for wellness and self-care.

Meditation is a mind-body practice that can bring in feelings of relaxation, and calm, grow self-awareness, and allows you and your children to learn mindfulness techniques you will carry throughout your life.

I highly recommend beginning a meditation practice with your children as soon as they arrive! Here are just some of the benefits of meditation for children and for you:

- 🦋 Better sleep
- 🦋 Relaxation
- 🦋 Family Wellness
- 🦋 Stress management
- 🦋 Self-regulation
- 🦋 More focused attention
- 🦋 Creativity
- 🦋 Better mood
- 🦋 Overall well-being
- 🦋 A more peaceful life

How do you teach a baby or small child to meditate? The answer is simple: model the behavior you want to see in your children.
Here are some ways to get started with meditation for babies and kids:

🦋 Start reading them these meditations before naps, bedtime, or during relaxing time.

🦋 Create mindful routines around bedtime that include these meditations or smaller pieces of them—perhaps even just deep breaths.

🦋 Read your kid's other books about mindfulness. Start with my Little Healers book series or other children's mindfulness books.

🦋 Allow your children to see you practicing meditation or deep breathing.

🦋 Please keep it simple. Start small by taking deep breaths together.

🦋 Allow your kids to move their bodies, fidget, or do whatever they need to while listening to these meditations. They are still absorbing all of it even if they are not sitting quietly.

🦋 Let go of expectations. Every child learns differently. Adjust how you use these meditations as your child needs shift and change.

🦋 When your child is old enough to read, have them read these out loud to you!

🦋 Listen to these meditations together on my website: www.beckypaynewellness.com and enjoy the practice of meditation together.

I hope you read these meditations with an open heart and mind.
I wish you peace and calm as your family moves through life together.

Kids Self Love Meditation with Positive Affirmations

Welcome to this guided meditation for self-love.
We will begin by relaxing the body and mind,
and you will hear me say positive affirmations.
You can repeat them silently to yourself or listen and relax.

Begin to feel your breath. Feel your breath move in and out of your body. As you breathe in, you feel your body expand. As you breathe out, let your body relax. Breathe in and feel your body expand. Breathe out, relax. Breathe in. Breathe out.

Feel your body relax now. Let these positive affirmations fill your mind as you relax.

I am relaxed.
I am peaceful.
I love myself.
I am kind to myself.
I accept myself.
I love myself exactly as I am.

I love my body.
I am confident.
I am kind.
I am loving.
I am love.

Listen and relax as I repeat those affirmations.

I am relaxed.
I am peaceful.
I love myself.
I am kind to myself.
I accept myself.
I love myself exactly as I am.

I love my body.
I am confident.
I am kind.
I am loving.
I am love.

Let yourself completely relax now as I repeat these affirmations one more time.

I am relaxed.
I am peaceful.
I love myself.
I am kind to myself.
I accept myself.
I love myself exactly as I am.

I love my body.
I am confident.
I am kind.
I am loving.
I am love.

Slowly return from this meditation by becoming aware of your breath. Breathe in, breathe out. Start to wiggle and move your body a little now. Take your time and slowly come back from this meditation.

Relax and Rest Meditation

Let's begin this meditation by relaxing. You can lie down if you want or be in any comfortable position. If you would like to get comfy with pillows and blankets, go ahead and do that now.
I am going to ask you to relax now.
Relax. Let your eyes close if you feel comfortable.
Wiggle your body a little to relax even more.
Let your body feel soft and heavy.
You are starting to relax.

During this meditation, I will say some things that will help you create a picture in your mind, and I will also name some body parts to help you relax.
Take a big breath in and a big breath out.
Take a breath in and another big breath out.
Keeping your eyes closed if you can,
begin to picture yourself on a beautiful
white fluffy cloud in the blue sky. It is a sunny, warm day.
The sun shines brightly down on you as you lie on the cloud.
You feel so comfortable and peaceful floating on this cloud.

The cloud moves very slowly.
You are warm, safe, and relaxed, floating on a cloud.
As you rest in your cozy cloud, you notice your feet.
Relax your feet. You notice your legs.
Relax your legs, and let them rest. Notice your belly.
Let your belly go. Relax. Notice your arms and hands.
Relax your arms and hands. Notice your face and head.
Relax your face and head. Your whole body is relaxed
as you peacefully rest on your cloud.
Let yourself relax here for a few minutes.

Slowly you start to come back to your cloud.
Notice how relaxed your body and mind feel.
Gently start to wiggle your fingers and toes
and begin to move your body slowly.
Take your time; when you are ready,
you can slowly sit up. You can return to
this meditation anytime you want to rest or relax.

Release Energy Meditation

Take a moment to get comfy. Grab any pillows or blankets to get extra cozy. You can sit or lie down, whatever feels best to you. Take a moment to get as comfortable as you can.

Close your eyes if you feel comfortable doing so, or feel free to leave them open.

Let's begin by becoming aware of your breathing. Can you feel your belly moving as you breathe in? Do you notice your belly relaxing as you breathe out? Let's take a few more deep breaths and try to see your belly moving with each breath.

Breathe in. Notice your belly. Breathe out.

Breathe in. Breathe out. Breathe in. Breathe out.

Now, let's release any energy that we don't need. If you are feeling sad or anxious, you could release that energy. If you fought with your friend, you could let that go now. Or you could release any energy in your body to calm down.

Start by placing your hands on your head. Move your hands from your head, down your body to your toes, or as far as you can without trying too hard. You can even make a noise as you move your hands- shoooooooo. Imagine that energy is leaving your body now.

Take a deep breath and place your hands on or around your head. As you breathe out, move your hands down your body, releasing energy. Shooooooo Two more times.

Breathe in, breathe out- shoooooo release energy.

Breathe in, breathe out-shooooooo release energy.

Now take a moment to notice how you feel. Rest and relax for the next couple of minutes.

Slowly start to bring your attention back to your breath and your belly. Notice your belly as you breathe in and out. Slowly begin to move your body by wiggling your fingers and toes. Open your eyes if they were closed. You can return to this meditation anytime you need to release energy.

Deep Breathing for Relaxation

Are you ready to relax with me? Will you breathe with me?

Get comfortable lying down or seated, whatever feels best for you. You can even get cozy with pillows or blankets. Let's start by relaxing your face. Let all the muscles around your mouth and eyes get very soft and relaxed. Close your eyes if you would like.

Take a few slow breaths. Slowly inhale through your nose. Slowly exhale out of your nose. Can you hear your breath? Can you feel your breath? Breathe in and breathe out with me.

Now place one hand on your belly and one hand over your heart. Take a deep breath in and feel your belly and chest filling up. Can you feel your hands moving out?
Take a deep breath out and feel your belly and chest go inward. Let's take five deep breaths together.
feeling your hands on your body as we breathe.
Take a deep breath in and feel your belly and chest filling up. Can you feel your hands moving out?

Take a deep breath out and feel your belly and chest go inward; empty all your breath out. Take a deep breath in and feel your belly and chest filling up.
Take a deep breath out and feel your belly and chest go inward.

Take a deep breath in

Take a deep breath out.

Take a deep breath in

Take a deep breath out.

Last one- Take a deep breath in

Take a deep breath out.

Keep your eyes closed, take your hands off your body, and rest. Notice how you feel. Do you feel calmer? Are you more relaxed? Taking deep breaths in and out can help you feel more relaxed whenever needed.

Bee Breath Meditation

We will be doing Bee Breath today! In this meditation, we will use our breathing to slow down and invite calmness into our bodies and minds. If you ever feel anxious, sad, or need to relax, this can help you calm down.

Take a moment to get into a comfortable position. You may want to sit on a pillow, cover up with a blanket, or sit with your legs crossed. If you wish, you can close your eyes or leave them open. Take a moment to get comfy now.
Is there anything else you need to get more comfortable with?

Bring your hands to your heart. Bring your palms together. Start to rub your hands together. Feel the warmth between your hands. Now, let your hands be still at your heart. Feel the warmth again.

Now as you breathe in, reach your arms up to the sky!
Reach your arms up high!

Then, as you breathe out, lower your arms to your sides.
Let your hands rest on your legs or wherever feels good to you.
Take a deep breath in, and as you breathe out, begin to hum like the sound of a bee. Hmmmmmmmmmm.

Breathe in and as you breathe out, keep your mouth closed and make the sound of a bee. Hmmmmmmmmmmm.
Breathe in, and fill your belly with breath.
Breathe out like a bee hmmmmmmmmm.
Breathe in, and fill your belly with breath.
Breath out. hmmmmmmmmmmmm.
Breathe in. Breathe out. Hmmmmmmmmmmm
Breathe in. Breathe out. Hmmmmmmmmmmm

Now, relax and breathe naturally without thinking about it.

Breathe in. Breathe out. Relax here for a few moments.

Slowly start to become aware of your breath again.
Notice how you feel. Do you feel calmer?
Maybe you feel more relaxed.

Gently start to move your body in any way that feels good.
If your eyes were closed, please open them now.

Bee breath can be very calming. Know that you can do this anytime you need to relax. You can do bees breathe for as many breaths as you would like. Simply breathe in and hum as you breathe out.

Guided Meditation to Relax Your Body

This meditation will help you relax your body.

Let's begin by lying comfortably or in any position that feels good. You can use pillows or blankets to make yourself as comfortable as possible. If you feel comfortable, close your eyes.

Take a few deep breaths. Breathe in. Breathe out. Breathe in. Breathe out. One more time, breathe in. Breathe out.

Bring all of your attention to your feet. Notice how your feet feel. Squeeze your feet. Squeeze your feet tightly. Hold this tension for two deep breaths.
Breathe in. Breathe out. Breathe in. Breathe out.
Release your feet. Relax your feet completely.
Take a deep breath in and out.

Bring all of your attention to your legs.
Notice how your legs feel. Squeeze the muscles in your legs. Squeeze your legs tightly. Hold this tension for two deep breaths. Breathe in. Breathe out. Breathe in. Breathe out. Release your legs. Relax your legs completely. Take a deep breath in and out.

Bring all of your attention to your belly. Notice how your belly feels. Squeeze the muscles in your belly. Tighten your belly. Hold this tension for two deep breaths. Breathe in. Breathe out. Breathe in. Breathe out. Release your belly.
Relax your belly completely. Take a deep breath in and out.

Bring all of your attention to your hands. Notice how your hands feel. Squeeze your hands into a fist. Tighten your hands. Hold this tension for two deep breaths. Breathe in. Breathe out. Breathe in. Breathe out. Release your hands.
Relax your hands completely. Take a deep breath in and out.

Bring all of your attention to your arms. Notice how your arms feel. Squeeze your arms. Tighten your arms. Hold this tension for two deep breaths. Breathe in. Breathe out. Breathe in. Breathe out. Release your arms. Relax your arms completely. Take a deep breath in and out.

Bring all of your attention to your face. Notice how your face feels. Squeeze the muscles in your face. Tighten your face. Hold this tension for two deep breaths. Breathe in. Breathe out. Breathe in. Breathe out. Release your face.
Relax your face completely. Take a deep breath in and out.

Bring all of your attention to your whole body. Notice how your body feels. Squeeze all the muscles in your whole body. Tighten your body. Hold this tension for two deep breaths. Breathe in. Breathe out. Breathe in. Breathe out. Release your whole.
Relax your whole body completely. Take a deep breath in and out.

Now keep your breath slow, steady, and relaxed. Take a couple of minutes to rest now completely. Slow, relaxed breathing while you rest.

Now become aware of your body again. You can wiggle your fingers and toes and gently start moving your whole body. Notice how you feel. You may feel more calm or relaxed.
This is a great meditation to do before naps or bedtime.

Chakra Balancing Meditation

Chakras are energy centers in the body. There are seven Chakras.
Each energy center holds a different type of energy.
We are going to balance our energy centers with this mediation.

Get comfortable lying down, seated, or even standing up.
Take a big breath in and a big breath out.

Now take an even bigger breath in and a long slow breath out.
One more time, a big breath in and a big breath out.

Let's begin with the crown chakra. Place your hands on top of your head.
Fill up the top of your head with purple light. Say to yourself, I am peaceful.

Now move your hands to your forehead. Fill up Your forehead with indigo light.
Say to yourself, I trust myself.

Move your hands to your throat. Fill Your throat with blue light. Say, "I speak confidently.

Move your hands to your heart. Fill Your heart with green light. Say, I love myself.

Move your hands to your tummy. Fill Your tummy with yellow light. Say, I am confident.

Move your hands under your belly button.
Fill the space under your belly button with orange light. Say, I am creative.

Move your hands to your hips. Fill your hips with red light. Say, I am calm.

Take your hands back to the top of your head and breathe in.
As you breathe out, move them down to your feet two more times.

Take your hands back to the top of your head and breathe in. As you breathe out, move them down to your feet.

Last time, Take your hands back to the top of your head and take a big breath in. As you breathe out, move them down to your feet.

How do you feel? Your chakras are now balanced! You can return to this meditation any time you need more balance or calm in your life.

Bedtime Meditation

Lie on your back with your hands on your belly. You may be lying in bed or anywhere that you feel comfortable. Make sure you are very comfortable. If you would like to, let your eyes close. Feel your hands on your belly. Take a big breath in and feel your hands lift as your belly rises and then sink as you breathe out

Now take your hands off your belly and let your arms lie by your sides, and we're going to imagine that instead of your bed, you are lying on a cloud.
A light, fluffy cloud that is so soft and comfortable. The cloud seems to wrap you up like a blanket.
You can feel the sun sending warmth to your cloud and your body as you lie on your cloud. Your whole body feels very warm and heavy. You are safe and supported lying on your cloud. Notice how your feet feel warm and heavy. Now notice your legs feeling warm and heavy. This relaxing feeling travels up your body into your hips and tummy. Your arms and your hands and your fingers feel warm and heavy.

Your chest and heart feel warm.
Your neck and your head are now warm and heavy.
Let your body relax into the soft, cozy, warm cloud.
You feel so relaxed, safe, and calm floating
on your cloud, so comfortable that you don't want to move.
You want to rest.

It feels so calming to rest your body. Now that your
body is relaxed, you can calm your mind, too.
Do you have any thoughts in your mind?
Imagine that the thoughts you have in your mind
start to float away with the breeze. See them slowly
leaving your mind and floating away with the breeze.
Relax your mind. Relax your body.
Notice how relaxed, safe, and calm you feel.

Now that you are relaxed, it is time for sleep.
Keep your eyes closed and your body and mind relaxed
as you drift off to sleep on your soft, safe cloud,
knowing you are peaceful, safe, and loved. Sweet dreams,
Little Healer!

Relax Your Body

Let's begin by taking a moment to allow your body to settle into a comfortable position. You could be lying down or seated. If you feel comfortable, close your eyes or allow them to relax. Today we will practice a short body scan; becoming aware of our bodies can help to calm our minds. Begin by taking a full breath in and a long breath out. Now bring awareness to the top of your body, become aware of your head, notice your face, and bring awareness to your neck and shoulders. Notice the top of your body.
Now moving down the body, notice your arms and hands. Become aware of your fingers.

Now notice your legs. Notice your upper legs, your lower legs, and your feet. Become aware of your toes.
Now begin to feel your back body.
Notice your back. Feel your back.
Now notice your front body.
Become aware of the front of your body.
Now become aware of your whole body.
Feel your entire body. Notice your entire body.
Rest for a few moments noticing your whole body.

Slowly begin to wiggle
your fingers and toes.
If your eyes are closed,
begin to open them.
Do you feel calmer?
Do you feel more relaxed?
How do you feel?
Body awareness meditation
is a great tool to calm
the body and relax the mind.

Loving Kindness Bedtime Meditation

Begin to get comfy in your bed. Wiggle around a little to get extra cozy. Let your eyes close if that feels good. Take a long, deep breath in. Take a long breath out and sigh as you breathe out. "Aaah!" Two more times.

Take a long, deep breath in.
Take a long breath out and sigh as you breathe out. "Aaah!"

Last one. Take a long, deep breath in.
Take a long breath out and sigh as you breathe out. "Aaah!"

You are now relaxing your body. Feel your body become soft and heavy like you are melting into your bed and feeling warm and cozy. You are completely safe and relaxed.

Now think about your heart. Feel your heart filling with warmth, love, and kindness. Let's begin with kindness for ourselves.
I will say three sentences, and you will repeat them silently in your mind. Think of these phrases in your mind:

May I be healthy.
May I be safe and protected.
May I be happy and peaceful.

Now we share our loving-kindness with our family. Picture your family in your mind. I will say three sentences, and you will repeat them silently in your mind. Think of these phrases in your mind sending them to your family.

May my family be healthy.
May my family be safe and protected.
May my family be happy and peaceful.

Now let's send loving kindness to all people and animals, even those we don't know. Let's send loving kindness to all beings.

May all beings be healthy.
May all beings be safe and protected.
May all beings be happy and peaceful.

Let yourself rest now in the energy of loving kindness for yourself, your family, and all beings!
Sweet dreams, Little Healer!

I hope you enjoyed reading these meditations
with your family, friends, or students.
If you have any difficulty, keep trying!
Release expectations of how you think meditation
"should" look and let your kids explore these
meditations in the ways that suit their
personalities best. If your children don't seem
responsive to them right now,
try again tomorrow or next week.
Every time you read them,
they absorb the information and become more mindful.
Keep practicing these meditations with them.

I hope these meditations become part of your daily life and establish a healthy foundation for wellness. Let's raise a generation of Little Healers together!

www.ingramcontent.com/pod-product-compliance
Lightning Source LLC
Chambersburg PA
CBHW050804220426
43209CB00089BA/1680